The Manager's Guide to Presentations

Ace your presentations and make your mark as a rising star in your organization

---

Lauren M. Hug, J.D., LL.M.

The Manager's Guide to Presentations

Copyright © 2014 Impackt Publishing

All rights reserved. No part of this book may be reproduced, stored in a retrieval system, or transmitted in any form or by any means, without the prior written permission of the publisher, except in the case of brief quotations embedded in critical articles or reviews.

Every effort has been made in the preparation of this book to ensure the accuracy of the information presented. However, the information contained in this book is sold without warranty, either express or implied. Neither the author, nor Impackt Publishing, and its dealers and distributors will be held liable for any damages caused or alleged to be caused directly or indirectly by this book.

Impackt Publishing has endeavored to provide trademark information about all of the companies and products mentioned in this book by the appropriate use of capitals. However, Impackt Publishing cannot guarantee the accuracy of this information.

First published: January 2014

Production Reference: 2100114

Published by Impackt Publishing Ltd.
Livery Place
35 Livery Street
Birmingham B3 2PB, UK.

ISBN 978-1-78300-014-2

www.impacktpublishing.com

Cover Image by Jarek Blaminsky (milak6@wp.pl)

Credits

Author
Lauren M. Hug

Reviewers
Karole Campbell
Erin Feldman

Commissioning Editors
Stephanie Moss
Danielle Rosen

Copy Editors
Jalasha D'costa
Maria Gould
Paul Hindle

Project Coordinators
Anurag Banerjee
Venitha Cutinho

Proofreaders
Maria Gould
Paul Hindle

Production Coordinator
Melwyn D'sa

Cover Work
Melwyn D'sa

Foreword

I remember my first official job interview like it was yesterday. Trying to find employment for any young kid just out of law school is tough, but it gets even tougher when you are seeking employment in the shadow of New York City. As I left to venture out into the great unknown, my grandmother looked at my suit and tie and politely told me that "you dress to impress." Taking the hint, I meekly returned to my bedroom, changed suits and ties and got the seal of approval. I did get the job, but I would like to think that it was on merit and not color coordination.

The world has changed since my grandparents were players in the business world, but the principles of success have not. You have to know your audience, define your goals, and sell your product, which, in this case, is yourself. This book provides all individuals—young and old, tired and true—with a blueprint of success.

The one thing that I have seen, repeatedly, over my business career is that so many people either do not truly know themselves or are afraid to make the introduction. As Lauren Hug so aptly points out in this book, if you are going to succeed in business, as well as in life, you must know yourself.

"The first thing you have to know is yourself," explained Adam Smith. "A man who knows himself can step outside himself and watch his own reactions like an observer." And isn't that the goal of any successful presentation?

Know your strengths, know your flaws, and know what can be corrected and/or modified. If you can see yourself through the eyes of those watching you, you will know what works and what flops; what attracts attention and what induces boredom.

As an attorney, I have had both the fortune and misfortune of sitting through a number of presentations. As this book explains, a one-size-fits-all approach does not exist in preparing for presentations. It is incumbent upon any speaker to do his/her homework. Who is your audience? What is the subject matter? Is humor fitting or out of place? Should I speak for a long period of time or should I be short, sweet, and to the point?

It is here that one must develop a presentation and Lauren has provided her readers with the ability to not only draft a blueprint, but execute it as well. Planning a presentation is typically intimidating and daunting, especially if it is a new concept. Not only must you put together something that is going to wow your audience, which may consist of bosses, customers, and dignitaries, but you then have to deal with the stress of making such a presentation.

Lauren breaks down the phobias that hinder successful presentations. By relating the building blocks of a successful presentation to the same building blocks most of us utilize in everyday life, Lauren has taken the idea of a presentation, which sometimes appears out of reach for people, and put it within an arm's length. This is the majesty of her book.

This book is a must read for any new manager entering the business world. This book is not about gimmicks, nor does it become a self-help book. This book is about success and it provides its readers with the tools they need to achieve such success. And if you read this book and take its message to heart, you will never have to picture another audience in their underwear again. That's how priceless this book is.

Joe Murray
Founder of the Murray Law Firm

About the Author

Lauren M. Hug, J.D., LL.M., an accomplished speaker, writer, and thinker, has helped people reach and motivate audiences for 20 years. For the past decade, she has applied analytical and communication skills to branding, messaging, and market research needs of businesses, big and small. As founder of HugSpeak Coaching & Consulting, she relies on presentation experience from the courtroom to the boardroom, involvement with dozens of corporate campaigns, insights from analyzing research along with cultural sensitivity from traveling and living abroad to advising clients in a wide variety of industries. Having discovered her gifts for public speaking, research, and strategy through her high school speech team, Lauren has a passion for helping students, as well as professionals, develop those crucial skills. Her positive, collaborative coaching approach has been described as empowering, life-changing, and even therapeutic. Lauren is an attorney and certified mediator whose academic credentials include an LL.M. with merit from the University of London, a J.D. with honors from the top-20 University of Texas School of Law, and a Bachelor of Journalism and Bachelor of Arts in Spanish from the University of Texas.

I would like to thank my eternally supportive husband Andrew for his patience with me while writing this book, my dear friend Craig Noack for his encouragement and excitement regarding this project, the savvy and energetic Karole Campbell for insightful feedback, the editorially gifted Erin Feldman for her expertise, the charming and brilliant Anna Rydne for camaraderie, and all the friends and family members who have cheered me along the way.

About the Reviewers

Karole Campbell owns Madwoman Marketing Strategies, a strategic advertising and marketing firm, and consults with diverse clients of all sizes across all industries including non-profits, utilities, education, entertainment, tourism, healthcare, and retail. She has presented to small audiences and large, her most recent a non-profit fundraising donation request to an audience of 500 plus.

Karole lives on a mountainside in Manitou Springs, Colorado with two manic and ancient border collies.

Erin Feldman is the founder of Write Right. She is a copywriter, editor, poet, and artist. She helps people and brands tell their stories. She has worked as a writer and editor for over seven years and has her MFA in creative writing and her BA in English and graphic design.

Contents

Preface	1
Chapter 1: Planning Your Presentation	**5**
The presentation planning process	6
Beginning with you	6
Addressing your concerns	6
Setting your own personal goal	8
Identifying your strengths	8
Assessing your personal brand	8
Leveraging your management skills	10
Knowing your team, knowing your audience	10
Understanding your boss	10
Connecting with your team	11
Getting to know the rest of the organization	11
Setting your presentation goal	12
What do you want the audience to do?	12
Brainstorming your goal	12
Refining your purpose	13
Presentation parameters	13
Length	13
Preparation time	13
Location	14
Technology	14
Audience size	14
Context	14
Summary	15
Chapter 2: Developing Your Presentation	**17**
What should you say in your presentation?	18
What does the audience need to know?	19
Think like your audience	19
Adapt to your audience	20
Why should your audience care?	20
Why should your audience act?	20
Why do you care?	21
Organizing your presentation	22

Opening	22
Appealing to the audience	22
Points (informing and persuading)	22
Call to action	23
Fleshing out your presentation	23
Types of content	23
A note about slides	24
Including the audience in your presentation	24
Introducing interaction	25
Summary	26

Chapter 3: Practicing Your Presentation   27

Speaking with authority	28
Posture	28
Gestures	28
Movement	29
Face	29
Eye contact	29
Voice	30
Rehearsing your presentation	30
Evaluating your rehearsal	30
Interactive rehearsal strategies	31
Independent rehearsal strategies	32
Preparing for Q&A sessions	34
Summary	35

Chapter 4: Giving Your Presentation   37

Before – Managing anxiety	38
Visualizing success	38
Visualizing worst-case scenarios	38
Pre-presentation checklist	38
During – Connecting with your audience	40
Relax	40
Greet	40
Smile	40
Make eye contact	41
Move	41
Interact	41
Be honest	41
After – Obtaining feedback	42
Discuss	42
Follow up	42
Evaluate	42
Summary	44

Preface

Congratulations on your promotion! As a new manager, there is a lot to learn and a lot of new duties to juggle. On top of all your responsibilities, you have to give your first presentation—a crucial step toward establishing yourself in your new role. This first presentation allows you to demonstrate your authority and share your leadership style. It also provides you with the opportunity to solidify relationships with your team members and your boss. It requires careful planning, thoughtful content development, sufficient practice, and confident delivery.

If that sounds like a lot to handle, don't worry! This book is here to guide you through the entire presentation process—from planning to writing to practicing to giving a masterful presentation that instills your team with confidence and enthusiasm. By following my practical, encouraging, and systematic approach, you'll be presentation-ready before you know it, prepared to impress key stakeholders, win over your team, and showcase your value to the entire organization.

We'll begin with some strategic thinking about your personality, audience, and purpose. An exercise designed to address any fears or anxiety will pave the way to identifying your own signature presentation style. Leveraging your management skills will help you understand your audience and define your presentation purpose. We'll also consider a variety of parameters that can impact the content and delivery of your presentation.

Like managing, presenting is about building relationships. A content development worksheet and a sample presentation outline assist you in pinpointing the information, arguments, and structure that will motivate the audience to act on your words. Several ways of sharing information and examples of interactive presentation techniques are explored, allowing you to choose the ones that match your style, audience, and purpose.

To ensure effective communication of your thoughtfully developed presentation content, the book contains a crash course in public speaking basics along with simple exercises to improve speaking skills. Several rehearsal strategies paired with an evaluation form empower you to select the practice method that fits your schedule and your presentation parameters. Handling Q&A can be tricky at times, so I've included some practical techniques and a "quick response" table for your convenience.

After all the strategizing, development, and practicing, the final chapter shows you how to approach the before, during, and after of your presentation. Stress-management techniques and a checklist of pre-presentation activities help you cope with anxiety and minimize uncertainty. Suggestions for staying focused and connected with the audience are also provided. A sample presentation evaluation form and recommended follow-up interview questions assist you in getting constructive feedback from key stakeholders to improve future presentations.

So, what are you waiting for? A management-worthy presentation is just a few pages away. Let's get started!

What this book covers

Chapter 1, Planning Your Presentation, begins with strategic thinking about your personality, audience, purpose, and parameters.

Chapter 2, Developing Your Presentation, will help you identify the information, arguments, and structure that will motivate your audience to act on your words.

Chapter 3, Practicing Your Presentation, will help you prepare to give a masterful presentation through rehearsing and evaluating your delivery and learning how to handle Q&A sessions.

Chapter 4, Giving Your Presentation, helps you manage stress, minimize uncertainty, stay connected with your audience, and follow up with key stakeholders as you navigate the before, during, and after of your presentation.

Who this book is for

This book guides readers through a practical, stress-free, step-by-step process of planning, developing, practicing, and delivering a masterful presentation. While specifically addressing the challenges new managers face when confronting their first presentation in a new role, the insights, exercises, and worksheets are ideal for anyone seeking to give a promotion-worthy presentation.

Conventions

In this book, you will find a number of styles of text that distinguish between different kinds of information. Here are some examples of these styles, and an explanation of their meaning.

New terms and **important words** are shown in bold.

Make a Note
Warnings or important notes appear in a box like this.

Tip
Tips and tricks appear like this.

Action Point
Action points appear like this

Reader feedback

Feedback from our readers is always welcome. Let us know what you think about this book—what you liked or may have disliked, or even if you have any questions. Reader feedback is important for us to develop titles that you really get the most out of.

To send us general feedback, simply send an e-mail to contact@impacktpublishing.com and mention the book title in the subject of your message.

If there is a book that you need and would like to see us publish, please send us a note via the **Submit Ideas** section of www.impacktpublishing.com, or send an e-mail to suggest@impacktpublishing.com.

If there is a topic that you have expertise in and you are interested in either writing or contributing to a book, you can also use the link or e-mail address above. One of our editors will get back to you within a week to discuss your idea further.

Piracy

Piracy of copyright material on the Internet is an ongoing problem across all media. At Impackt, we take the protection of our copyright and licenses very seriously. If you come across any illegal copies of our works, in any form, on the Internet, please provide us with the location address or website name immediately so that we can pursue a remedy.

Please contact us at copyright@impacktpublishing.com with a link to the suspected pirated material.

We appreciate your help in protecting our authors, and our ability to bring you valuable content.

Planning Your Presentation

As a new manager, you have a lot on your plate. You have to learn your new role, identify your leadership style, figure out how you fit into the organizational culture, and meet and connect with every member of your team, just to name a few.

Great news! Thoroughly planning for your first presentation will help you accomplish all of these things.

An effective presentation requires you to know yourself, your audience, and your purpose. This chapter will help you to:

- Complete the presentation planning process
- Begin with you: identify your fears, goals, strengths, and personal brand
- Know your team, supervisors, and organization
- Set presentation goals by defining your presentation purpose
- Consider all presentation parameters

Let's get started!

The presentation planning process

Finding the time to craft an effective presentation in the midst of all your new duties can be daunting. The **Presentation Planning Worksheet** included in this section helps to break up the planning process into simple steps that can be completed independently whenever your new schedule allows.

Take a moment to familiarize yourself with the Presentation Planning Worksheet. As you work your way through the chapter, each section will be explained in detail, and you will be prompted to record your progress and answers in the corresponding sections. When completed, this worksheet will contain all the information you need to prepare an effective presentation.

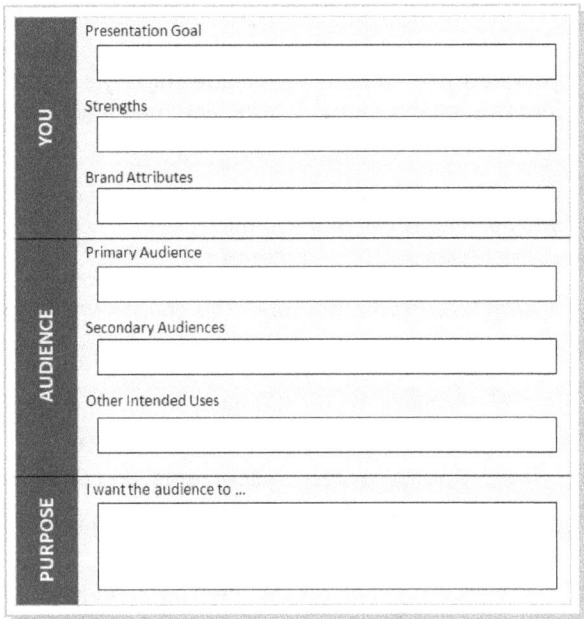

Beginning with you

Your perspective, *your* strengths, and *your* personality are all reasons you were hired for your new position. You need to rely on them to deliver presentations that will establish your position in the organization, demonstrate your unique skills and abilities, reinforce your authority, motivate your team, and impress your superiors.

A confident presentation begins with addressing any concerns or anxieties you have about speaking. The next section will help you conquer your fears about presenting.

Addressing your concerns

If you've never had any fear or anxiety about public speaking, go ahead and skip to the next section. If the mere thought of this presentation has you gnawing at your fingernails or losing sleep, then this section is for you.

Planning Your Presentation

Don't let nerves or anxiety keep you from preparing and delivering a fantastic presentation! Go ahead and talk about them. What are you afraid of? What is waking you up in the middle of the night? What is creating knots in the pit of your stomach?

Vague worries are far more powerful than specific, named concerns. Using this chart and the following steps, we'll send those fears packing:

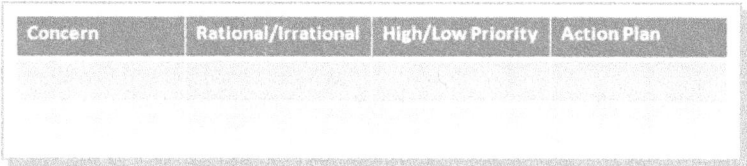

1. Name your concerns; write down everything that is stressing you out!
2. Define whether each fear is rational or irrational.
3. Recognize the irrational fears and release them. Don't waste time and energy on something that won't happen.

Make a Note

A **rational** fear is something that is likely to occur. It's rational to be worried about losing your footing and falling while speaking; it happens all the time. An **irrational** fear is something that's unlikely to occur. It's irrational to fear that your boss will fire you for performing poorly on one presentation.

---

4. Prioritize the rational fears.
5. For each rational fear, ask yourself, "So what? So what if I fall? So, what if I forget everything I was going to say?"

    The answers to these questions will help you decide where to focus your energy. If you fall, a quick acknowledgment or a funny comment will get your presentation back on track. But, if you forget everything you were planning to say, your supervisor could be mightily displeased. Prioritization makes it clear that you should spend more time working on what you're going to say than worrying about falling on your face.

6. Develop a plan for attacking the rational fears.

Some fears are easy to address with simple problem-solving. If you're afraid of falling, wear shoes and clothes that allow you to move freely and maintain your balance. If you're afraid of having toilet paper stuck to your shoe, plan to do a quick wardrobe check before showtime. Releasing fears related to crafting and delivering an effective presentation will require more planning. That's exactly what this book is here to help you do, so keep reading!

By naming your fears, analyzing them, and developing a plan for handling them, your presentation will demonstrate the confidence and problem-solving skills that are key to successful management.

Setting your own personal goal

What do *you* want to get out of this presentation? I'm not talking about the **presentation purpose** discussed in the *Setting your presentation goal* section later in this chapter. Rather, what do you hope to accomplish *personally*?

Do you want to demonstrate that you are a capable problem-solver? Do you want to establish yourself as a leader? Do you want to gain the respect and admiration of your team? Do you want to confirm that you were the right choice for the job?

Maybe your goals are all of the above and more, but choose the one that is most compelling to you. Write it down in the designated spot on the Presentation Planning Worksheet found in the *The presentation planning process* section at the beginning of this chapter.

Identifying your strengths

What are the talents, skills, and abilities that got you promoted to or hired for this position? Do you excel at analyzing data and forecasting trends? Are you relational, intuitive, and good at encouraging people? Are you practical and able to break a problem down into easily manageable pieces? What do you do better than your co-workers or peers?

Jot down three key strengths on the Presentation Planning Worksheet. Building a presentation around these strengths will allow you to feel comfortable, reinforce your unique contributions to the organization, and connect with your new team.

Assessing your personal brand

One of the key elements of an effective presentation is authenticity. Being real, being you.

Unfortunately, a lot of presentation "tips" and "rules" prevent people from being themselves. That's why so many presentations are bland, boring, and torturous. Everyone is copying and mimicking the same tired routine. Most presentations waste precious time by including unnecessary information and too many slides with uninspired images and far too much text. Typical presentations lose sight of the fact that every slide and every piece of data should be aimed at engaging the audience.

Newsflash! You aren't any other presenter. You have your own leadership style, management personality, and approach to team dynamics. Embracing what is unique about you is what will help you stand out from the crowd. More importantly, your presentation won't be credible if your presentation persona is vastly different from the way you communicate every day.

So, who are you? Let's do a quick personal branding exercise:

Who Do You Think You Are?	How Do Others See You?	How to You Want to Be Seen?
Personal Brand Attributes		

1. **Who do you think you are?** Write down five to eight adjectives that describe who you are all the time—with your best friend, your boss, or a person you just can't stand.
2. **How do others see you?** Ask your friends or family members to list adjectives describing you. Look over work reviews to see which adjectives frequently occur. Ask your boss and your team. Write down the five to eight words most commonly used by others to describe you.
3. **How do you want to be seen?** Write down five to eight adjectives that describe the way you want others to perceive you.
    ➢ Look across all three columns on the Personal Branding Chart and work through the following steps until you've identified five distinct words that describe you.
    ➢ Circle words that appear in every column. Write them in the Personal Brand Attributes box. If you've identified five distinct words, you can skip the rest of the steps.
    ➢ Circle words that appear in the last two columns. Write them in the Personal Brand Attributes box. If you've now identified five distinct words, you can skip the next step.
    ➢ Circle words that appear in the first and last columns. Write them in the Personal Brand Attributes box. If you haven't identified five distinct words by this point, fill the remaining spots with words from the last column that best describe how you'd like to be seen.

When you've identified five distinct words, you've identified your personal brand attributes.

Identifying these attributes helps you create a presentation style that is authentically you. A funny, smart, artistic, ambitious, and brave person presents differently from someone who is serious, thoughtful, empowering, resourceful, and innovative.

Write your five personal brand attributes on the Presentation Planning Worksheet. They'll be useful in *Chapter 2, Developing Your Presentation*.

Leveraging your management skills

As you transition into your new role, your management skills will come in handy while planning your first presentation. Getting to know your boss, your team, and your organization provides the perfect opportunity to gain an understanding of your presentation audience or evaluators. Additionally, the same goal-setting tools you use to define the direction of your team can be leveraged to create clear and specific objectives for your presentation as well.

This section will guide you through getting to know your audience while also getting to know your organization. Then, you'll work through the process of setting a goal for your presentation.

Knowing your team, knowing your audience

A successful presentation meets the audience's needs and addresses the audience's interests in a way that resonates with them. To deliver a presentation that moves people to action, you have to know your audience.

As a new manager, you have to get to know several internal audiences, and fast! By connecting and interacting with key players in the organization, you can establish your role and gain an understanding of your presentation audience at the same time.

Will you be presenting to internal groups such as your team, your boss, high-level executives, or the board of directors? Will you be presenting to external groups such as customers, clients, or the media? Perhaps you are presenting to some combination of these or other groups.

Chances are, unless you're in a position that involves media or customer relations, most of your presentations will be given to internal audiences. We'll look at three likely internal audiences—your boss, your team, and internal strategic partners—and discuss ways to connect with them. Then, we'll talk about identifying and prioritizing the audiences for this particular presentation.

Understanding your boss

Every presentation you give in your new role will impact your immediate boss in some way: not only will your boss evaluate your presentation, but your performance will also reflect on them. It is important that you understand your boss's expectations so you can craft a presentation that resonates with them and with other executives.

Find an opportunity to briefly talk with your boss and ask the following questions:

- What are your goals for this presentation?
- Do you have any requirements or preferences regarding style and delivery?
- What do you hate to see in presentations?
- Can you describe an example of a strong presentation?
- What life will the presentation have beyond the delivery itself?

By understanding your boss's goals, you'll be able to address the issues he or she finds most worthy of discussion. Likewise, avoid anything your boss expressly disapproves of in a presentation.

Connecting with your team

As you get to know your team, listen carefully to their views on meetings and presentations. Ask them about organizational norms for presentations including any formatting or technology requirements. Ask them what they like to see in a presentation and the approaches that best hold their attention. Ask them what kind of examples and illustrations help them to understand and act on information.

Getting to know the rest of the organization

Succeeding in your new position will require an understanding of organizational norms and expectations regarding your role. Your first presentation as a new manager may be the first time members of other departments see you in action. Learning and adhering to the accepted organizational procedure for presentations demonstrates your adaptability, flexibility, and commitment.

Also, observe the culture. Chat with people from other departments about presentations that have been particularly well received, as well as those that have been considered a disaster! Ask if they have any "pet peeves" about ways that presenters from outside their department provide information to them. Seeking the input of those outside your immediate team allows you to quickly build strategic internal partnerships and cement yourself in your new role.

Make a Note

When speaking to an external audience, check for organizational knowledge about the audience by gathering additional information online.

Once you've done the background work of connecting with and getting to know key internal stakeholders, it's time to identify your audience for this specific presentation.

Let's say your boss intends to watch you present to your team about upcoming projects. Your primary audience is your team. The presentation is for their benefit, so you will need to focus on making sure that the content and delivery resonates with them.

Your boss is a secondary audience. While the information isn't for their benefit, they will be listening, observing, and making judgments about how you are performing in your new role. So, it's important to consider their perspective when preparing the presentation.

Let's further assume your presentation will be recorded and sent throughout the organization. This is yet another audience, and a successful presentation should be designed to communicate to this broader group as well.

Use the Presentation Planning Worksheet from the beginning of this chapter to record and prioritize the audiences and uses of this presentation.

Setting your presentation goal

As a new manager, you're in charge of setting goals and objectives for your team. As with any project, in your presentation you need to set a goal that is clear, achievable, and measurable. The success of any presentation is measured by whether the audience hears, receives, and acts on that message.

What do you want the audience to do?

How many times have you left a presentation or a speech wondering, "What was the point of that? Why did I sit through it?" It happens all the time because presenters fail to clearly set a goal.

To illustrate the importance of defining the presentation purpose, let's consider the following hypothetical situation: imagine you work for a cell phone manufacturer that has a new product coming out. You will be speaking about the product. You could talk about features, price, development, innovation, partnerships, and so on, but if you try to cover everything, the audience will be overwhelmed or bored and nothing will stick.

How do you narrow your focus? You must decide what you want the audience to do.

Should they:

- Understand the features on the new phone?
- Be excited about the features on the new phone?
- Buy the new phone?
- Tell people about the new phone?
- Know where the company is in the development process of the phone?

Each possible purpose is slightly different, requiring different information, different stories, and different tones.

Brainstorming your goal

Reflecting on the "cell phone launch" example from the previous section, think about your own presentation and answer this question:

What do you want the audience to do when you finish speaking?

Jot down whatever comes immediately to mind. Now let's examine your answer.

Is it clear?

The purpose must be easy to understand and something you can articulate in a simple sentence. For example, *I want the audience to* _____.

Is it achievable?

The goal must be something you can accomplish with *this* audience and the time you've been given. Aim for a strategically-selected, tangible outcome.

Is it measurable?

Most organizations are results-oriented, and managers that consistently demonstrate success are highly valued. For that reason, your goal should be specific enough to allow you to determine whether it was achieved. It's more difficult to measure feelings and impressions than actions. So, "I want the audience to tell three people about the product" is better than "I want the audience to be excited about the product." Not only does a measurable goal enable you to track your effectiveness and communicate it to your bosses, a measurable goal also ensures you will give the audience actionable directives.

Refining your purpose

Rethink and rephrase your goal until you can answer yes to all of the preceding questions. Then, give the purpose two final tests: does it align with your boss's expectations? Is it clear enough to give your audience actionable direction?

If your goal aligns with expectations, provides actionable direction to your team, and is clear, achievable, and measurable, plug it into the Presentation Planning Worksheet and move on to considering presentation parameters.

Presentation parameters

Congratulations and breathe a sigh of relief! You've made it through the heavy thinking, but there are still some little details to consider that can make a big difference to your presentation success.

Take a moment to consider the following factors and the ways they might impact your presentation:

Length

The length of time you've been given to speak dictates how much material and detail you can cover in your presentation. Remember to allow time for questions and interaction and stick to time limits. Nothing you have to say is more important than your audience's time.

Preparation time

Multi-tasking is an important part of being a manager, so you can't allow this presentation to take an inordinate amount of your time and attention. No matter how much you want to include Pixar-caliber animation, whiling away the hours designing world-class slides is probably not the best use of your time.

Location

Where will you be presenting? If possible, visit the location well in advance of your presentation to get a feel for the space, the acoustics, and any unique features that can hinder or enhance your delivery. Figure out the seating arrangements and determine whether you will be sitting or standing while speaking. Note the technological options available in the room and inquire as to whether any audience members will be conferenced into the presentation. If visiting is not a possibility, find out as much about the space as you can. It is better to know than to be surprised.

Technology

Technology enhances many excellent presentations, but it is also the cause of many a presentation nightmare. Don't use technology just because everyone else does it. Carefully consider if technology will help you achieve your presentation goal. And, if you choose to use technology, be sure you have a back-up plan in case something goes wrong. It's terrible to spend hours crafting a beautiful slide deck only to discover that the laptop won't boot or the file won't open. It's downright horrific if you aren't prepared to give the presentation anyway!

Audience size

A small group lends itself to a more conversational approach with lots of audience interaction. A very large crowd requires a delivery style that will reach the back row.

Context

Considering the circumstances surrounding your presentation will allow you to craft content and a delivery style that will maximize audience attention and responsiveness. Will your presentation stand alone or will it be part of a series? Will you be introduced by someone else or will you need to include your own introduction? What time of day will it be? Will people be hungry? Tired? Itching to call it a day?

Summary

In this chapter, you have:

- Developed a plan for conquering any presentation fears
- Articulated your personal goal and unique strengths
- Discovered your personal brand attributes that define your presentation style
- Established connections with key stakeholders within your organization
- Identified and prioritized the audiences for your presentations
- Defined a clear, achievable, measurable, and actionable presentation purpose that will meet your boss's expectations
- Considered parameters that will impact decisions about how to craft your presentation
- Completed the Presentation Planning Worksheet for use in *Chapter 2*

Let's move on to the next chapter where you'll develop your presentation!

>2

Developing Your Presentation

By now you should have completed the Presentation Planning Worksheet from *Chapter 1, Planning Your Presentation*. In this chapter, you'll use the worksheet as a springboard for crafting persuasive presentation content that will solidify your role as a new manager, motivate your team to follow your lead, and convince your audience to act.

In this chapter, you'll learn how to:

- Identify what you should say in your presentation
- Organize your presentation in a way that promotes understanding
- Flesh out your presentation with audience-appropriate methods of sharing and demonstrating
- Be prepared to include the audience in the presentation

By the end of this chapter, you will have drafted your entire presentation and developed ways of reinforcing the content. You'll then be ready to practice your presentation, gaining an ease and confidence with the material that will allow you to connect with your team, bosses, and other audience members.

Developing Your Presentation

What should you say in your presentation?

As we discussed in *Chapter 1, Planning Your Presentation*, a successful presentation accomplishes its purpose by getting the audience to hear, receive, and act on its message. That means the *purpose* and the *audience* must be your focus as you prepare your content.

As a new manager, you have to communicate in ways that resonate with your team members and bosses. As you develop your presentation content, think about everything from their perspective. What do they already know about your topic? What do they need to know? What will they find most persuasive? How do they process information? How do they prefer to be engaged?

Take a look at the **Content Development Worksheet below**. We'll be using this to work through the process of drafting your presentation. As you can see, purpose and audience(s) are at the top. Fill in those blanks with the *purpose* and *audience(s)* you defined and identified in the last chapter.

	CONTENT DEVELOPMENT WORKSHEET
PURPOSE:	
AUDIENCE(S)	WHY THEY SHOULD CARE
PRIMARY:	
SECONDARY:	
KEY MUST-KNOW INFO (3-6 FACTS):	
WHY AUDIENCE SHOULD ACT (3-6 REASONS):	
WHY YOU CARE:	

We'll work on filling in the rest of the worksheet as we consider the information (facts) and arguments (reasons) that will resonate with your specific audiences.

What does the audience need to know?

A concise review of relevant factors such as data points, key players in the organization, or project history is crucial to establishing context and driving action. However, deciding how much background information is necessary or how many basic facts to include can be tricky. This first presentation lets your team and bosses know what to expect from future meetings and group interactions. You don't want to talk down to your audience or waste too much precious time on material that is already familiar. On the other hand, you don't want to talk over their heads and lose them by assuming knowledge they don't have.

Assume your presentation purpose is to convince your audience to make a change to a product design. How do you know how much information to provide and what topics to cover?

Think like your audience

Recall conversations with any members of your *primary* audience and review any notes. Now, take out a blank piece of paper and brainstorm everything your primary audience needs to know to act on the purpose. Given your new role, the audience will undoubtedly need to know something about your background as well as your vision for your team, the project at hand, and how the project serves the organization as a whole. Other relevant material might include cost considerations, project history, key players, target markets, or competitive analysis. To convince your audience to change a product design, for example, you'll need to explain the importance of the change, the available options, the costs/benefits of each option, your recommended course of action, and the reasons supporting it. You'll also need to address how your proposed course of action will impact the other current projects and workload of your team.

Take a moment to consider your brainstormed list from the perspective of your secondary audiences as well. This is especially important if your secondary audiences include your boss, board members, or other decision-makers, since they are responsible for evaluating your performance. With a proposed product change, your boss may be concerned about budget and resources, while the finance department may be more interested in the net value of the recommended course of action. Are there any key pieces of information that should be included in your presentation to address their needs and expectations? If so, add them to your list.

Now that you've considered all the information needs and concerns from the perspective of your audience, you should identify the key content areas to emphasize. Circle all the pieces of information that are not common knowledge among your audience. Prioritize them by highlighting any information that your audience *must know*. This is the compelling information that your audience needs in order to be convinced to act, and therefore it should be the focus of your presentation.

Action Point
Based on the preceding exercise, write down three to six of the most important things your audience must know on the Content Development Worksheet.

Adapt to your audience

As a new manager, you want to keep your team engaged and enthusiastic, but there is always the possibility that you will encounter boredom or confusion because of the lack of or overabundance of facts in your presentation. You should prepare for this scenario by building flexibility into your presentation and developing strategies for responding to your audience.

Attention and adaptability are key to surviving any crisis. As you are speaking, watch your audience for signs of disconnection or discontent (such as fidgeting, lack of eye contact, confused expressions, or whispering), and don't be afraid to ask questions like:

- ➤ Have I lost you? Which part was confusing?
- ➤ Do you already know this? Should I skip past this part?
- ➤ What do I need to discuss more thoroughly?

Ways of proactively including your audience will be discussed in more depth later when we delve into establishing an audience connection while speaking, but it's never too early to wrap your mind around the possibility of going "off-script" in order to meet the needs of your audience.

Why should your audience care?

Facts and information aren't enough to convince an audience to listen and act. The same motivational skills that help you manage your team will help you show the audience why they should care about your message. How does the topic of your presentation impact the audience personally?

Positive reasons are usually more compelling than negative ones. Sure, you may be able to frighten your audience by pointing out that their jobs depend on their response to your presentation, but in the long term, building camaraderie, ownership, and a sense of pride in one's work will not only result in a more enthusiastic presentation response, but will create a harmonious, productive energy that extends into all your managerial activities. For example, pointing out that the implementation of the proposed product change allows your team to play a key role in organizational success by driving a 30 percent increase in Q3 sales is more effective than forecasting a Q3 loss in the absence of any change.

Action Point

On the Content Development Worksheet, write down one or two reasons why the audience should care about your presentation.

Why should your audience act?

Consider the "must-know" facts that you will be sharing (the three to six facts you wrote down on your Content Development Worksheet). What values, emotions, or aspirations of your audience can be linked to those facts?

For example, let's say your presentation purpose is to get the organization to green-light your team's plans for a new product. You're planning to share these "must-know" facts: it's made from recycled materials, it's completely unique, and it will cost significantly less than competing products. To convince your audience of the product's worthiness, you need to present reasons that will resonate with them. An audience that values green-technology will be convinced by environmental arguments. An audience that strives for innovation will be motivated by emphasizing creativity and cutting-edge advances. An audience primarily interested in profit will be persuaded by explanations of increased market share and scalability.

Linking "must-know" information to compelling, audience-specific values provides your audience with reasons to act, and creates engagement and motivation.

Action Point

On the Content Development Worksheet, write down three to six reasons why the audience should heed your presentation's call to action.

Why do you care?

Have you thought about why you actually care about this presentation? When I ask coaching clients why they care about their presentations, the answer is often, "I don't know" followed by a variation of "It's part of my job." That response will never convince an audience to act.

Audiences can sense a lack of conviction, disinterest, or dishonesty in a presenter. To deliver an effective presentation, *you* must be convinced of the relevance and importance of the message. As a new manager, this presentation is your first opportunity to showcase your passion and vision for your team, your project, and your organization. Identifying the specific reasons you care about this topic will provide you with conviction as you acclimate to your new role. It's okay to be honest and share with the audience your desire to prove your worth and abilities. Honesty is humanizing and fosters connection.

Look at your list of "must-know" information again. What stories, values, and emotions resonate with *you* regarding those facts? Sharing the reasons you care about the presentation reinforces all the reasons the audience should care and creates even more incentive for them to follow-through on your call to action.

Action Point

On the Content Development Worksheet, write down the one main reason you care about the purpose of your presentation.

As you can see, the time you spend building relationships with your audience prior to the presentation is invaluable. It demonstrates your commitment to the organization, establishes your conviction about your presentation's purpose, and enables you to think about the presentation from the audience's perspective. This results in increased engagement and follow-through by your team—all signs of a successful presentation!

Organizing your presentation

All this thinking and brainstorming has served a purpose. In the midst of all your new responsibilities and activities, you've thought of everything you need to successfully put your presentation together. Take your Content Development Worksheet and write the answers into this simple template:

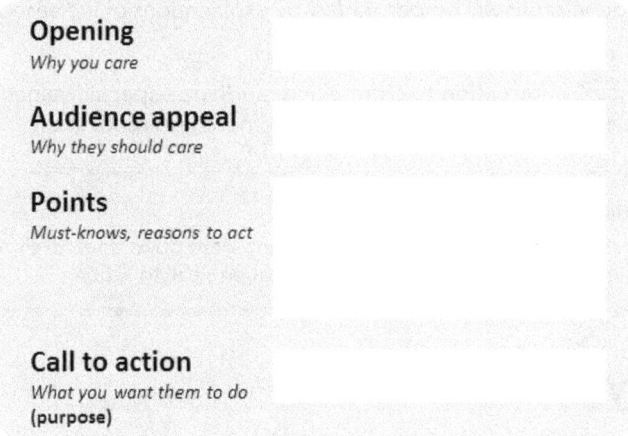

Opening

Some presenters put a lot of pressure on themselves to have a show-stopping opening. However, poorly executed "show-stoppers" alienate the audience instead of engaging them. Unless you are a skilled comedian or showman, skip the jokes and pyrotechnics and opt for the personal touch instead. As a new manager, this is the perfect opportunity to open your presentation with a compelling personal story that explains why you care about its purpose.

Appealing to the audience

Early on in your presentation, you should explain to the audience why the content should matter to them. Focus on encouraging and empowering terminology.

Points (informing and persuading)

Now comes the body of your presentation: your key points. These are the audience "must-knows" and the reasons to act (from your Content Development Worksheet) organized into an engaging flow:

- Pair your reasons with corresponding or supporting facts. Try to consolidate them into roughly three main points.
- Think about the order in which these key points should be presented. Does one logically precede another? Is one more compelling than another?

- If there is a clear logical progression to the points, order them accordingly.
- If a logical progression isn't required, always lead with your strongest point to ensure that the audience will absorb the most important content.

Call to action

Finally, your presentation should conclude with exactly what you want the audience to do. This is the presentation purpose you defined in *Chapter 1, Planning Your Presentation*.

And there you have it. The bare bones of your presentation are now compiled in an organized, easy-to-follow template.

Fleshing out your presentation

With the skeleton of your presentation in place, you now need to put meat on the bones by carefully considering how your audience processes information. Is your new team composed of visual, auditory, or kinetic learners? Do your bosses like to go into the details or do they prefer to see the big picture?

Include content that engages, clarifies, explains, and demonstrates. Avoid anything that isn't geared toward convincing the audience to act.

Tip

Funny anecdotes are superfluous and distracting if they don't relate directly to your presentation purpose.

Types of content

This presentation is an excellent opportunity to demonstrate that you have listened to your new team members and bosses and that you understand how to effectively communicate with them. Think creatively about the kinds of content that will effectively make your point to *this* audience. To help you with your brainstorming, here is a non-exclusive list of potential ways of fleshing out your presentation:

- **Stories and examples**: Clarify abstract concepts by providing a relatable, real-world context
- **Demonstrations**: Allow the audience to observe and experience with their own eyes
- **Illustrations/charts/graphs**: Break complex information into smaller pieces or digestible visual components
- **Lists**: Highlight keywords, concepts, or steps

Which content types will work best for your presentation purpose and with your specific audience? Go back to your basic outline and expand it to include at least one content type for each section or point. Make sure each addition is targeted to accomplishing your purpose.

Your time (and the attention span of your audience) is limited, so you probably won't be able to present all the content included in your presentation draft. However, thinking about examples and aids for every point enables you to identify the most important and compelling aspects of your presentation. It also equips you to answer potential questions or to address areas of audience interest that you might not have anticipated otherwise.

A note about slides

You may have noticed that I haven't mentioned PowerPoint or any other presentation programs yet. There's a reason for that. Despite the near universal rush to start a PowerPoint document when faced with a presentation, slides are not synonymous with presentations. *Slides are not content.* Slides are merely one method of communicating.

An effective presentation is planned and prepared long before the presenter sits down to create a slide deck. That's why we've walked through the process of planning and developing your first presentation without considering presentation software. By focusing on your audience and purpose (and *not* the pre-programmed formats and limitations of PowerPoint), you have sketched the contours of a presentation that will effectively fulfill the audience's expectations of you as a new manager. Maybe you've even realized that your presentation will be better without a deck. Slides have become so ubiquitous in presentations that audiences often immediately tune them out. When preparing your content, consider whether another method of communication will convey your point more effectively. Whiteboards, flipcharts, props, hand-outs, and short audio/video clips all provide you with dynamic, adaptable, and unexpected ways of communicating information and engaging the audience at the same time.

If you must use slides, do your best to follow these rules of thumb:

- **Use slides sparingly**: Only include slides that are absolutely necessary to accomplish your presentation purpose.
- **Limit the amount of text on each slide**: Avoid complete paragraphs and sentences. Think in terms of keywords.
- **Never read your slides out loud**: Pause to let your audience read slides for themselves or omit the slides and speak the words.
- **Avoid complicated animation that requires precise timing**: A live presentation is unpredictable. You don't want to lose your audience while rewinding or fast-forwarding through unnecessary animation.
- **Don't rely on your slides as a crutch**: Technology failures are routine. Be ready to give your presentation regardless of whether the computer or the projector cooperates.

Including the audience in your presentation

Did you ever sit mindlessly through a classroom lecture, daydreaming and doodling on your notebook as a professor droned on and on? Being talked *at* is an alienating, boredom-inducing experience that is unlikely to produce understanding or action. Even the most well-planned and well-prepared content can become a monotonous stream of indistinguishable sounds if care isn't taken to include and interact with the audience.

Don't be that professor! Build audience interaction into your presentation to keep people engaged and on track.

Introducing interaction

Many presenters fear audience interaction because it's unpredictable and unknown. Introducing interaction, though, is a safeguard against your audience tuning out. It also creates trust and encourages audience members to buy into your purpose. Perhaps more importantly, inviting your audience to participate, especially in your first presentation in this new role, invokes a sense of confidence in your position and establishes you as an open and empowering leader.

Let's briefly look at several ways of including an audience in a presentation:

- **Rhetorical questions** keep the audience mentally engaged without risking a runaway train of comments and potentially off-topic discussion. When you ask a question, your vocal inflection naturally changes and your audience instinctively searches their brains for an answer.

- **Polling the audience** encourages members to mentally and physically engage by raising their hands to answer your questions. These questions typically start with the phrase "How many of you …" When used strategically, polling the audience is a quick, non-threatening way to take the pulse on various issues.

- **List-making** gives the audience the opportunity to speak up within a limited scope. This approach works especially well for covering background information or bringing everyone up to speed. For example, ask the audience something like, "What were the most successful projects of last year?" Record the answers on a whiteboard, flipchart, or slide. You can increase the interactivity by inviting discussion about the responses, if you are so inclined.

- **Empowering an audience member** to explain background information or give a recap of key factors demonstrates that you value and trust the contributions of others. It also adds variety and interest to the presentation since you won't be the one doing all the talking.

- **Open-ended questions** allow audience members to freely speak their minds in response to a targeted inquiry. The thoughts and contributions of peers or superiors often prove to interest and engage audiences.

- **Incremental Q&A sessions** allow audience members to seek clarification and bring up additional information immediately after the relevant portion of the presentation. When audience members are aware that questions will be welcomed throughout the presentation, they are more likely to stay engaged.

The following chart compares the predictability, interactivity, and best use of each method:

Method	Predictability	Interactivity	Best Use
Rhetorical Questions	High	Low	Works well for presenters nervous about audience getting off-track and in very large groups where discussions aren't practical.
Poll the Audience	High	Medium	Works well for presenters nervous about audience getting off-track and in very large groups where discussions aren't practical.
Make a List	Medium	High	Works well in small- to mid-sized groups and in presentations where there is time to record (and potentially discuss) the answers.
Empower Audience Member	Medium	High	Works well with small- to mid-sized groups. Will also work in a larger group if the question is carefully streamlined and asked of a member whose answer is relatively predictable.
Ask Open-Ended Questions	Low	Very High	Works best in smaller groups where discussion is possible, and you have the ability to thoroughly address any unexpected answers.
Incremental Q&A	Low	High	Works in any size group, as long as each Q&A session is promptly closed when time has expired.

To keep your audience engaged and invested, aim to include at least two of these methods of including the audience. And don't be afraid to invent your own ways of encouraging audience participation. Remember, whatever gets your audience to heed your call to action is worth trying!

Summary

In this chapter, you have:

- Identified what you should say in your presentation
- Organized your presentation into a template
- Developed engaging ways of explaining, demonstrating, and bringing your presentation content to life
- Carefully considered the role that slides will play in your presentation
- Explored engaging alternatives to the standard slide deck
- Selected at least two methods of encouraging audience participation

In the next chapter, we'll talk about ways of practicing your content in order to ensure that your first presentation as a new manager is a success.

> 3

Practicing Your Presentation

As a new manager, your first presentation is about more than just the words you say. It's about the impression you leave on your team, your boss, and other audience members. They will be looking to see if you exude leadership, authority, and communication skills, as well as the ability to motivate and think on your feet.

With all the responsibilities facing you in your new role, you don't have a lot of spare time to practice your presentation. This chapter will provide you with quick, effective ways to polish your public speaking skills, become confident delivering your material, and handle questions from your team and bosses with aplomb.

In this chapter you'll learn how to:

- ➤ Speak with authority
- ➤ Rehearse strategically and effectively
- ➤ Prepare for Q&A sessions

By the end of this chapter you will be ready to deliver a presentation that inspires your team and confirms your leadership role.

Speaking with authority

The previous chapters have led you through the process of developing targeted content for your first presentation as a new manager. The way you deliver that content, though, s the key to establishing yourself as the leader your new role requires you to be.

As a manager, practicing and honing public speaking skills is an essential part of your on-going professional development. You will increasingly be called upon to speak in public situations. Given the newness of your role, it's normal to feel apprehensive or uncertain about the tone to strike when addressing people looking to you for leadership and direction (especially if you've only recently met or been assigned to manage them). No matter how you feel internally, though, you must look calm, confident, and in control during your presentation. Your demeanor sets the tone for future interactions.

You must look and sound like a confident, capable, enthusiastic team leader. Your posture, gestures, movement, face, eye contact, and voice all communicate your position of authority and tell the audience how they should respond to you. This section will help you make sure you are sending the right message.

Posture

One of the fastest and most effective ways to demonstrate confidence and authority is to stand up straight. Pulling your shoulders back and keeping your head level establishes you as fearless, open, and ready to engage your audience. To maintain your balance, plant your feet shoulder-width apart and stand your ground. Avoid rocking, swaying, shuffling your feet, slouching, or looking down at the ground or up at the ceiling. Aside from being distracting for the audience, they are signs of unease and anxiety.

Action Point

Posture exercise: Stand in front of a full-length mirror and deliver the opening to your presentation. Observe your shoulders, head, back, and feet. What does your posture say about you? Now, plant your feet, pull your shoulders back, and keep your head level. Notice how this posture instantly makes you appear more authoritative.

Gestures

Part of your new role entails setting goals and keeping people on task. Powerful, controlled gestures indicate the deliberation and attentiveness required to manage follow-throughs. Unfortunately, gestures tend to cause concern for many presenters. The key to powerful and purposeful gestures isn't extensive and intricate choreography; it's becoming aware of and putting a stop to weak and nervous gestures such as hand-clasping, fidgeting, and arms frozen at your sides. To overcome preoccupation with your hands, consider occupying them with the task of holding a glass of water or a pen.

Practicing Your Presentation

Action Point

Gesture exercise: Utilizing the posture from the previous exercise, stand in front of your smartphone or webcam and record yourself delivering the "audience appeal" portion of your presentation. Watch the recording, paying close attention to your gestures. Now, hold your hands at hip-height with your palms up. Record yourself as you try controlled, open, and inviting gestures by widening and narrowing the space between your hands.

Movement

Meaningful movement around the room or across the stage is another way to demonstrate the focus and discipline necessary for keeping multiple team members motivated and on task. Aimless pacing or wandering undermines your authority as a manager and distracts your audience from your message. Standing frozen in one spot (or worse yet, behind a lectern) makes you look timid and afraid. Transitions between thoughts or presentation sections provide logical opportunities to move to a new spot and address every corner of the room. Audience inclusion and interaction portions should also contain planned movement throughout the room.

Action Point

Movement exercise: To ensure purposeful movement, review your presentation template from *Chapter 2, Developing Your Presentation*, and mark specific times for moving across the room or through the audience.

Face

Facial expressions send myriad of non-verbal messages to your audience. You want to be sure your face isn't communicating a message you don't intend to send. Aim for animated, vibrant expressions such as smiles and widened eyes that keep your audience engaged with the content of your presentation. Avoid furrowed brows, frowns, or blank stares. These are apathetic, ignorant, or angry expressions that evoke negative emotional responses.

Action Point

Facial exercise: Utilizing the posture and gestures from the previous exercises, stand in front of a mirror and deliver the points of your presentation. Watch your facial expressions and note anything that fails to convey managerial authority. Match your facial expressions to the response you want to evoke.

Eye contact

Boldly looking your audience in the eye is the presentation equivalent of a strong handshake. It creates a connection and establishes you as direct, confident, and unwavering. During the presentation, pick at least two to three people to focus on until you are warmed up and comfortable fixing your gaze on the audience as a whole.

Action Point

Eye contact exercise: Stand in front of a mirror and deliver the "call to action" portion of your speech while looking directly into your own eyes.

Voice

Present yourself as a leader by speaking loudly, clearly, and at a moderate speed. Every person in the room should be able to hear your voice and understand your words. Be aware of any mush-mouthed tendencies or combinations of words that trip up your tongue. Avoid over-pronunciation, too. Unless you routinely speak with perfect diction, over-pronunciation can sound stilted and overly formal. Strive to keep your tone strong and even, avoiding signs of anxiety such as a quivering or shaking voice. Vary your speaking rate to keep things interesting, highlight important information, and connect with the audience. Don't be afraid to pause. Planned silences demonstrate control and confidence. They also provide your audience with an opportunity to process information and catch up.

Action Point

Vocal exercise: Record yourself practicing your entire presentation. Play it back, listening to the strength of your voice, the clarity of your diction, and the speed of your delivery. Practice until you sound strong, clear, and conversational.

Rehearsing your presentation

While the public speaking skills covered in the last section are an important aspect of delivering a presentation worthy of your new status, mastering the specific material at hand is a crucial step toward establishing yourself as a leader within your organization. Sloppy, rambling, unprepared, and unrehearsed presentations are unprofessional, inconsiderate, and an inefficient use of the time and talents of other members of the organization. Sufficient rehearsal enables you to speak with authority, streamline your delivery, and complete your presentation within the allotted time. As a new manager, delivering a polished, well-prepared presentation will underscore the professionalism, attention to detail, and effective time management you expect from your team.

Evaluating your rehearsal

To ensure your success at conveying managerial excellence through your presentation, evaluate (or have others evaluate) your rehearsal efforts on the basis of the following six key factors:

1. Connection
2. Clarity
3. Confidence
4. Preparedness
5. Fluency
6. Leadership

The following **Evaluation Form** will aid you in recording, comparing, and measuring the feedback you obtain on each of these factors when following the suggested rehearsal strategies. This form can be used to evaluate rehearsals of future presentations as well, providing you with the ability to track feedback on your presentation skills over time and flag areas for sustained focus or improvement.

METRIC	EVALUATION AND COMMENTS
Connection (How well does the presenter relate to the audience?)	
Clarity (How clearly does the presenter explain the content?)	
Confidence (How well does the presenter convey control of the situation?)	
Preparedness (How well does the presenter know the material?)	
Fluency (How clearly does the presenter speak?)	
Leadership (How well does the presenter convey authority and leadership?)	
Other (What else did the presenter do well or should the presenter improve upon?)	

Interactive rehearsal strategies

Rehearsing in front of a practice audience is the most data-rich way of evaluating the effectiveness of your presentation skills. As the target audience for your presentation, a practice audience composed of eventual audience members will provide you with the most direct and actionable feedback. Additionally, soliciting their input and constructive criticism gives you more opportunities to build rapport in a one-on-one or small group setting. Asking for their opinion demonstrates that you care, you listen, and that you will act upon their suggestions. As a new manager, though, you may be reluctant to allow team members or bosses to watch your presentation in the rehearsal stage. Other options for practice audience members include professional contacts outside of your organization or people with whom you have personal relationships.

Obviously, a start-to-finish run-through of your complete presentation including slides, demonstrations, and anything else you plan to present gives you first-hand experience of delivering your content. If at all possible, try to conduct the run-through in the actual space where the real presentation will take place. Strategically recruit three to five team members (those you need to spend more time with, need to win over, or have already identified as smart and insightful) or a handful of thoughtful professional or personal contacts outside your organization. Give them copies of the evaluation form so they can jot down their observations and suggestions as you are presenting. Detailed verbal feedback after the run-through would be helpful, but just watching the presentation can require a considerable time commitment. The evaluation form allows you to use uniform metrics and save your practice audience members some time.

Respecting the time, workload, and other obligations of workplace associates (especially your boss) will often mean you won't be able to rehearse your presentation in its entirety with them. Here are some other ways to practice your presentation and solicit valuable feedback with a smaller time commitment from your practice audience.

Coffee conversation

Schedule a coffee or lunch date with one or two practice audience members and talk through your presentation in an informal, conversational way. Solicit their verbal feedback and follow up by sending them the evaluation form to gather and track additional thoughts and comments.

Section run-through

Ask for 15 minutes of a practice audience member's time and do as thorough a run-through as possible of one portion of your presentation. This is an excellent way to get feedback on the parts of your presentation that you are most nervous about. Allowing them to complete an evaluation form will provide you with insights about the specific section and your overall delivery.

Executive summary presentation

An effective and efficient way of rehearsing for your boss, an executive summary presentation is a stripped down, top-line taste of the material you plan to present. Go through the highlights and deliver this mini-presentation in less than 10 minutes, then pay careful attention to the feedback your boss provides.

Independent rehearsal strategies

Finding time to rehearse with practice audiences can be a challenge when faced with a packed schedule and a significant learning curve regarding all your new duties and responsibilities as a manager. Independent rehearsal strategies allow you to practice your presentation in your own time, while still tracking progress and identifying areas for focus or improvement. Use the evaluation form with the rehearsal strategies below, trying to evaluate your performance from the perspective of your target audience.

Mirror run-through

Similar to many of the public speaking exercises discussed earlier in this chapter, practicing your entire presentation in front of a mirror allows you to make sure your posture, movement, face, and eye contact are representative of your new leadership position. It also allows you to become familiar with the material and helps you commit large portions of the presentation to memory without actively memorizing specific words or sections.

Audio run-through

Talk your entire presentation into an audio recorder and evaluate how confident, clear, enthusiastic, motivating, and authoritative your voice sounds. Identify any overuse of "ums" or other words you unconsciously say too frequently. When you record a version you feel good about, listen to that recording over and over again to master the material.

Video run-through

Film your entire presentation including slides, demonstrative aids, and anything else you plan to present. Watching the video will allow you the greatest opportunity to evaluate your performance because you can stop and re-watch sections that need special attention. A video run-through is also useful for soliciting the feedback of practice audience members who cannot be present at an in-person run-through.

Regardless of the rehearsal strategies you choose, practicing your presentation develops the confidence and authority you need to demonstrate your mastery of the material and your fitness for your new leadership role. Use the following chart to help you decide which strategies best fit your rehearsal needs by comparing how well they simulate the actual presentation, the accuracy and depth of feedback they provide, the amount of time they require, and the ease of scheduling the rehearsal session in light of required logistics and other people involved.

	Closeness to Real Thing	Accuracy of Feedback	Depth of Feedback	Time Requirement	Ease of Scheduling
Full Run-through	High	High	High	High	Hard
Video Run-through	High	High	High	High	Easy
Section Run-through	Medium	High	High	Low	Medium
Executive Summary	Medium	High	High	Low	Medium
Mirror Run-through	High	Medium	Medium	Medium	Easy
Audio Run-through	Medium	Medium	Medium	Medium	Easy
Coffee Conversation	Low	Medium	High	Medium	Medium

Preparing for Q&A sessions

By honing your public speaking skills and rehearsing for your presentation, you will now be equipped to present yourself as a competent, confident, inspirational new manager. An element of unpredictability, however, is inherent in any presentation. Preparation cannot control the way the audience responds and reacts. Furthermore, any traction you gain due to a flawless presentation will evaporate if you have difficulty fielding questions from your team, bosses, or other audience members.

Questions can pop up at any time during a presentation. Don't assume that the omission of a formal "question and answer" session on your presentation assignment means that questions won't be asked. Demonstrate your leadership skills, your comprehensive understanding of your presentation subject matter, and your ability to think on your feet by preparing yourself to handle questions whenever they arise.

Make a list of inevitable or predictable questions likely to be raised in response to your presentation material. Questions posed by your practice audience members are a good place to start. Prepare answers to these questions in much the same way you developed your presentation content in *Chapter 2, Developing Your Presentation*, then practice your delivery of those answers using the rehearsal strategies covered in this chapter.

Unpredictable questions tend to be more troublesome. Fortunately, rehearsing a handful of responses will enable you to handle unexpected or off-topic questions with the confidence of a seasoned manager. In the following table, you will find a variety of unpredictable question scenarios and sample responses to aid you in addressing them with confidence:

SAMPLE RESPONSES TO UNEXPECTED QUESTIONS	
When you don't know the answer ...	<ul><li>I don't know, but I'll find out and get back to you.</li><li>I don't have the data with me right now, but I'll send you a copy later today.</li><li>You know a lot about that area. What do you think?</li><li>Who would like to share their thoughts on that?</li></ul>
When the question confuses you ...	<ul><li>I'm not certain I understood the question. Could you rephrase?</li><li>Could you elaborate on that?</li><li>Does anyone else share a similar concern?</li></ul>
When the question is off-topic ...	<ul><li>How does that relate to our topic today?</li><li>That's beyond the scope of our discussion today, but let's talk about it some more when we're done here.</li><li>Excellent question. I think it merits further exploration. Would you like to take the lead on developing an answer?</li><li>Great topic for another presentation!</li></ul>

Summary

In this chapter you have:

- Polished the public speaking skills that will help you present yourself as a leader
- Evaluated and mastered your presentation by rehearsing in front of practice audiences or by yourself
- Prepared to handle Q&A sessions with confidence and authority by practicing answers to expected and unexpected questions

In the next chapter, you'll learn how to tackle the moments leading up to your first presentation as a new manager, how to stay connected with your audience during the presentation, and how to solicit constructive criticism and follow-up with team members and key stakeholders.

Giving Your Presentation

Presentation time is almost here! You've planned, developed, and practiced your material. Now is the time to wow your team and bosses by delivering a presentation that informs, motivates, and sets the tone for your new leadership role.

In this chapter you'll learn how to:

- Manage anxiety *before* your presentation
- Connect with the audience *during* your presentation
- Obtain feedback *after* your presentation

By the end of this chapter, you will have delivered a presentation that solidifies your new management position through confident leadership, authoritative public speaking, relationship-building with your team, and strategic follow-up with key organizational stakeholders.

Before – Managing anxiety

Hopefully, with all the work you've already done to prepare for your presentation, you are feeling confident about the big day. As the presentation approaches, however, you may find yourself feeling a little uncertain. The anxiety management strategies in this section will help you overcome any nerves that could undermine your managerial authority.

Visualizing success

A tried-and-true method often utilized by professional athletes, success visualization calms you and reminds you that an impressive, effective presentation is within your reach. When anxiety threatens to get the better of you, mentally rehearse your presentation, imagining the successful delivery of every word, gesture, demonstration, and answer. Visualize what you will look like and feel like as you confidently move about the room, communicating your vision, inspiring your team, and showcasing your leadership capabilities.

Visualizing worst-case scenarios

Another approach to combating nerves and uncertainty is imagining potential presentation flaws or setbacks while mentally rehearsing your presentation. Similar to the "conquering your fears" exercise in *Chapter 1, Planning Your Presentation*, visualizing worst-case scenarios allows you to mentally plan for potential problems, recognize that they aren't that threatening, and develop a strategy for coping with them should they arise.

What is causing you the most anxiety as the presentation draws near? Name that fear, and then consider what the likely outcomes are if it actually happened. As you encounter each imaginary setback, visualize yourself rising to the challenge, addressing the problem, and successfully continuing with your presentation. By igniting and relying on your problem-solving skills, you'll be able to re-conceptualize the presentation as a hands-on, pragmatic project and team-building activity instead of merely a public-speaking task.

Pre-presentation checklist

Live speaking is always rife with uncertainty, but you can manage anxiety by taking control of all the things within your power. Using the advice and strategies in this book, you've already exercised a considerable amount of control through planning, developing, and practicing your presentation. In the last 24 hours before you are scheduled to speak, make a detailed checklist of everything you'll need to bring and do to deliver a confident, successful presentation.

For example, the *day before* the presentation, you should gather all the materials and tools you'll need (or anticipate needing) in one convenient place. Organize your notes, visual aids, and hand-outs in chronological order. Include extra copies as backups or in case additional people decide to attend the presentation at the last minute. Likewise, include both an electronic and hard copy of your presentation so you'll be prepared to share your content no matter what technological disasters may befall you. Among other things, you should also select and try on your clothing, practice your presentation, review your schedule for the following day, and get a reasonable amount of sleep.

On the *day of* the presentation, set the stage for success. Activities should include running a thorough technology check, energizing your body with proper nutrition, and warding off a dry throat or mouth with a strategically placed source of water. You may also want to include one or two visualization exercises on your list.

Immediately before you begin speaking, meet your team and other audience members at the door, welcoming them and thanking them for their attendance. Your list should also include reminders to prepare your voice and collect your thoughts.

The following **Sample Pre-Presentation Checklist** provides a starting point, but be sure to create your own list, adding items specific to your presentation, your new role, your team, and your organization:

Sample Pre-Presentation Checklist

The Day Before
- ❑ Gather all presentation materials in one place
    - o Electronic and hard copies of your presentation deck
    - o Handouts, notes, visual aids (arranged in the correct order)
    - o Tools like flip-charts, dry erase markers, pens, and scratch paper
- ❑ Select, try-on, and practice your presentation while wearing your entire presentation outfit
- ❑ Review your schedule to make sure you have allotted enough time for dressing, grooming, travel, and set-up
- ❑ Get enough sleep

The Day Of
- ❑ Check technology to make sure everything is working
- ❑ Eat an energizing meal or snack an hour or so before your presentation time
- ❑ Stash a bottle or cup of water in a place that will be easily accessible during your presentation
- ❑ Do some quick visualization exercises

Immediately Before
- ❑ Enthusiastically greet audience members
- ❑ Take a small drink of water
- ❑ Find a brief moment to collect yourself

During – Connecting with your audience

While you practiced your presentation in the last chapter, the focus was on *you* – making sure *you* looked and sounded like a rising leader within your organization. During your presentation, however, *the audience* must be your sole focus. To persuade your team to adopt your message, you have to create a connection that compels them to listen and act on what you have to say. The following diagram and explanations outline a strategy for creating that connection:

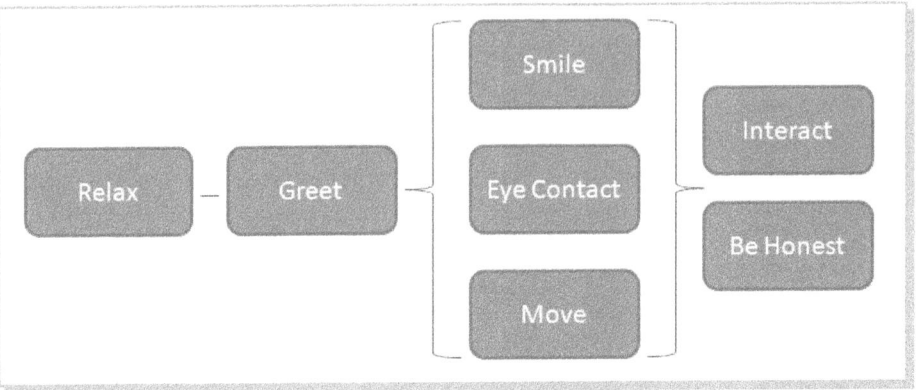

Relax

To connect with your audience, you have to forget about yourself and make them your number one priority. At the outset of your presentation, take a deep breath and let go of all the little things you worked on during the rehearsal stage. At this point, any worry or doubt about your gestures, speaking style, or command of the material will only drive a wedge between you and your audience. On the other hand, an attentive presence and enthusiastic embrace of this unique opportunity to build a rapport and consensus among your team members is a fail-proof way to showcase your confident leadership skills and demonstrate you are the right person for your new role.

Greet

As we discussed in the last section, begin connecting with your audience immediately before your presentation by shaking hands and saying hello as team members and supervisors enter the room. Greeting your audience allows you to further solidify new relationships with organizational players as well as spend a little face-time with key stakeholders. Engaging in casual conversation before addressing the larger group will also help you feel more comfortable, conversational, and spontaneous. It has the added benefit of warming up your voice and preparing you to speak.

Smile

A smile puts others at ease, demonstrates your interest in connecting with them, and instantly energizes both you and the audience. Even a forced smile is better than no smile at all, because it establishes you as approachable and makes you appear willing to engage.

Make eye contact

In *Chapter 3, Practicing Your Presentation*, you were encouraged to practice this fundamental public speaking skill while rehearsing your presentation. When you are in front of your real audience, start by focusing on two or three friendly faces—perhaps people who acted as a practice audience for you or those you connected with during the pre-presentation greeting—and expand to include every member of the audience. Avoid scattering your gaze by engaging with one person per sentence or thought. Try to make eye contact with every key player at least once during your presentation. It will make your team members feel included and valued by you.

Move

Movement keeps your audience energized and allows you to connect with every corner of the room. In *Chapter 3*, you identified places for movement within your presentation template and practiced those movements during rehearsals. If, however, you find yourself forgetting your plan, don't panic. Simply move in a manner that includes all audience members. After you've stood for a while on one side of the room, cross to the other side in order to engage with everyone in attendance. Physical command of the room will put your team members at ease and reassure them that they are in capable hands.

Interact

As you smile, make eye contact and move around the room; watch for expressions and body language that indicate your audience is tracking with you. In *Chapter 1, Planning Your Presentation*, we discussed the need to adapt your approach if your audience seems to be losing interest. Make use of the audience interaction activities that you brainstormed while planning your presentation. Include team members directly by referencing comments or conversations that occurred during the greeting period, rehearsals, or other discussions. Answer questions as they are asked, or use one of the sample responses from *Chapter 3* as a way of deftly deflecting while validating the asker and keeping them engaged in the presentation.

Be honest

Sometimes a presentation *will* fall flat. If all of the previous methods of connecting with your audience appear to be failing, win them back with brutal honesty. Don't be afraid to acknowledge their confusion or boredom with bold statements such as:

- I seem to have lost you. Where did I stop making sense?
- That didn't come out right. Let me try again.
- Some of our team members are experts in this area. Would any of them like to weigh in?

Acknowledging a bit of imperfection in an otherwise thoughtful, planned, and practiced presentation is humanizing and winsome. It demonstrates that you aren't afraid of confronting difficult situations and are able to devise new strategies for dealing with them. People respond to and follow *people*, not robotic, off-putting perfection.

After – Obtaining feedback

When you've finally made it through your entire presentation, you'll probably feel either exhilarated or exhausted! Either way, resist the urge to retreat to your office to celebrate and unwind. To get the most out of your presentation in terms of management experience, team-building, and professional development, soliciting feedback is an important wrap-up activity. Information-gathering at this stage allows you to identify areas of consensus, capitalize on momentum, and evaluate your performance as both a presenter and a new manager.

Discuss

Gather informal feedback about your presentation immediately after you finish speaking by casually asking which points had the most traction, which aspects of your delivery style were particularly effective, and what actions team members plan to take in response to your message. Jot down key findings or repeated observations and comments for future reference.

Follow up

Continue engaging with your team and other audience members by following up on any unanswered questions, loose ends, or areas for further exploration. Through e-mail or spontaneous conversations, provide additional information or opportunities to discuss your presentation material, as well as implications for the organization. Along with the information and discussion topics, invite informal feedback by asking open-ended questions such as:

- What part of the presentation did you find most useful?
- What one thing should I focus on improving for future presentations?
- What captured your attention the most?

Evaluate

For in-depth feedback, solicit a more formal evaluation from your boss and a few key team members. Schedule 15 – 30 minutes to review your performance, discuss strengths, identify weaknesses, and develop action plans for moving forward. The following **Presentation Evaluation Form** corresponds to the metrics identified in *Chapter 3, Practicing Your Presentation*. Use it to compare your rehearsal efforts with your actual presentation, to track improvement, and to solicit actionable feedback in the event that scheduling a post-presentation debrief with key stakeholders isn't possible.

Presentation Evaluation

Rate the following factors on a scale of 1-10

POOR (1)   EXCELLENT (10)

Factor	1	2	3	4	5	6	7	8	9	10
Connection with audience	1	2	3	4	5	6	7	8	9	10
Clarity of material	1	2	3	4	5	6	7	8	9	10
Confidence	1	2	3	4	5	6	7	8	9	10
Preparation	1	2	3	4	5	6	7	8	9	10
Clarity of speech	1	2	3	4	5	6	7	8	9	10
Leadership skills	1	2	3	4	5	6	7	8	9	10

Other comments:

Suggestions for improvement:

With your first presentation as a new manager successfully behind you, look for any themes that emerge from the feedback regarding your presentation topic, delivery style, or leadership approach. The information you obtain will help you manage current and future projects related to your presentation topic, better connect with and serve your team, and deliver effective presentations every time you are called upon to speak.

Summary

In this chapter you have:

- Managed pre-presentation anxiety and uncertainty
- Connected with your audience during your presentation
- Obtained feedback on your presentation content, delivery, and overall effectiveness

Congratulations! You've conquered your first presentation as a new manager!

By embracing your unique speaking style, understanding your audience, crafting a presentation that meets the needs of key stakeholders, and practicing superior public speaking skills, all your presentations as a new manager (and beyond) are certain to exceed expectations.

www.ingramcontent.com/pod-product-compliance
Lightning Source LLC
Chambersburg PA
CBHW080925170426
43201CB00016B/2268